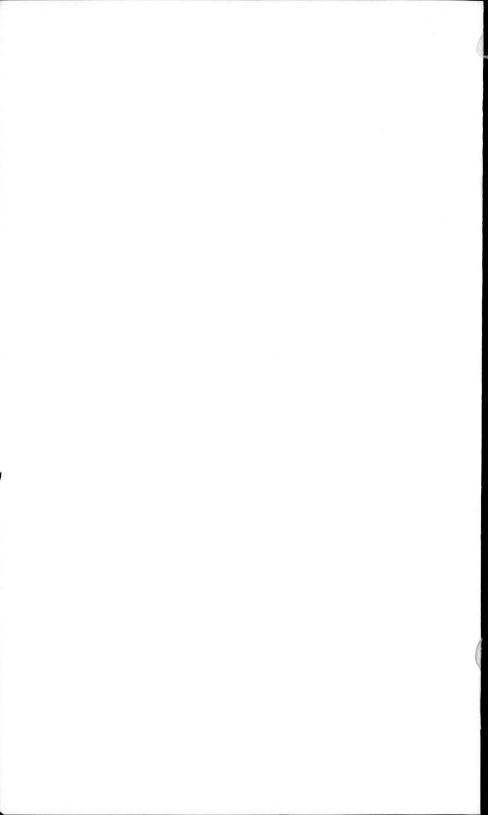

THE SILENT REALITY

CHANCE HANSEN

ISBN: 978-1-4669-0005-9 (sc)
ISBN: 978-1-4669-0006-6 (hc)
ISBN: 978-1-4669-0007-3 (e)

Library of Congress Control Number: 2011917952

Trafford rev. 10/24/2011

 www.trafford.com

North America & international
toll-free: 1 888 232 4444 (USA & Canada)
phone: 250 383 6864 ♦ fax: 812 355 4082

Contents

Acknowledgments

I would like to thank the Creator . . . for giving me wisdom and the understanding to be able to help others as well as helping me through life's trials.

To my Mom (Pascha Hansen) . . . for teaching me all that I know and for supporting me in every way and in every decision that I have made. Without the decisions that Mom made I wouldn't be where I am today.

To Granny (Gisela Hansen) . . . for the encouragement and for helping me with all the long days and late nights of editing.

To my whole family my Mom, Granny, and Granddad (Harold Hansen) . . . for being there for me and making this the family that I am proud to be part of and for the love that we have for each other.

To Mrs. Rouga Swereda . . . for all the late night phone calls when we needed help, having faith in me, your caring and honesty about my stories,

To Aunt Karen . . . for all your support, encouragement and for believing in me that I could do it.

A special thanks to all that have supported, helped and been there for me through the years.

To the person that is reading this book thank you for your support.

The Unspoken Side

Red with anger,
Controlled by fear.
Mental abuse, verbal abuse,
To them it's never wrong.

Always right,
Never wanting to lose.
Standing up for yourself,
Might mean getting a bruise.

Wanting to give up,
But afraid to leave.
Pretending you're somewhere else,
It's yourself you deceive.

Tired of hearing their lies,
Taking the blame for their rage.
Feeling small and useless,
Like a mouse in a cage.

They argue like children,
On a merry go round.
Abused people living this way,
Are afraid to make a sound.

Forever Loved

I SPOTTED YOU AT THE OTHER end of the gym and my heartbeat quickened. I became nervous when we met unexpectedly at the beverage table, unsure of what to say, I turned around and stiffly walked out of the room into the empty hall. The hall seamed as dead and dreary as the sky above the school. I cleared my throat trying to remove the lump of nervousness. I wished that I was able to walk without fearing my knees would buckle. I pushed the exit door to the outside to see the clouds beyond the tree line obscuring the late evening sun which gave the horizon a mixture of reds, purples, and blues. The silence was only broken by a woodpecker's tapping and the school yard was like a ghostly view of mixed memories as I sat on the front steps of the school. I put my head on my knees, angry with myself for what I couldn't and didn't do.

A rhythmic beat and laughter from within the school echoed into the open air as someone came outside and then closed the door. High heels clicked as they walked toward me. She sat down beside me staring at the horizon with me. I glanced at Cynthia's red dress almost as if hypnotized by how it glimmered in the ever-so-slowly darkening sky.

"I-I wish that we were more than friends." I said fighting to control my nervous stammer.

Cynthia's parents considered me worthless, and the popular students hated the friendship that was between the two of us. I looked behind us toward the door to see a few members of the lacrosse team spying on us through the door. I truly wished there was a way that I could be alone with her.

Within the week Cynthia transferred from school for good and as the days accumulated into years we ran into each other once before my marriage failed. As time continues to pass by I still wonder if there was a chance for us. Whenever I try to look you up on-line, you seem to have vanished. I ask myself if there had been something between us, or if I could have done something differently in my life. Truly all the past is now gone and whatever I had in my life has vanished or changed beyond recognition. If Cynthia walked through that door now I wish the past could be brought back from the ashes of that imploded building. Truly I wish I could replay the past again to be able to have the fun that we had.

Would you love me the way I loved you if we were together again? If we met again could we go back in time and continue from where we left off?

Gaming for the Mind

Asking innocent questions strikes fear into the most troubled soul. The helpless follow their every spoken word as if their word is law. Breaking completely away from their mind games is nearly impossible. Being called useless and foolish draws you closer to them, not in love but in support, to help you live a mentally unhappy life, although you say nothing is wrong. They come up with the worst outlooks on life if you make your own decisions or walk away from their life. They criticize any fault that they find in you, even if it was a mistake that you made years ago. You are also accountable for any mistakes that they themselves have made although you haven't done anything wrong. Believing you are at fault is the most dangerous mental mistake that holds on for years.

Their given rage is a strangled love like an emotional pot, that shifts and churns like boiling stew. Unable to give up to the guilt over unnecessary lectures from the mastermind gives you stress, and mental pain, like a flooding bathtub. As a mastermind they play with your emotions of fear, guilt and sympathy, until you take the blame for a car wreck or for anything else that they can blame on you, all the while avoiding the acceptance of fault.

Masterminds control your decisions by beating you down to your knees and looking down on your beliefs, belittling your thoughts, and crushing your dreams. All of your life the mastermind has changed you and you will continue to deny the problem until you can no longer find another open door. Life becomes hopeless as the world becomes smaller while the corrections become larger. You feel alone, betrayed by friends and family who were once there and now have vanished into the wind. Feeling like no one is around to help you stand on your own, just like the first time you rode a bicycle.

Fighting with the accuser will only bring pain to those that always feel accountable for others mistakes no matter what the action. The mastermind's battle takes its victory over the young in mind and heart and eats on the forgiving, and those that are unable to stand on their own. When standing like a dying flower, the petals droopingly dangle like apologies and tears of guilt. All those that live in their hand don't see the happenings of the clues while the acid is eating away at the gloss and finished surface within. Lost within the meaning of love, vulnerable to the thoughts of others who haven't seen the bend in the road, you feel as if they don't see the puppeteer the way you do. They expect you to know better although they don't expect you to know anything.

You are as strong as the words you use, and how you use them, for nothing else is more persuasive or powerful. What can shake someone to the core more than words of anger or words that reveal a blindfold that is covering your eyes from the truth? Those with a light in their eyes are blindly following their strict voice, hoping that it will lead them to where the spotlight is located, rather than walking in a circle of arguments that continually point out the imperfections of your past actions. Even if broken from the spell, the damage is that of an earthquake, never to be the same again. The aftershocks will continue time and time again. The destruction is so great that the heart and mind have lost their voice but they too will return from the ashes over time!

Destructive and degrading words are like a crowbar tearing the planks off of the crate that holds your heart.

Those that control others can't control themselves.

Trial of Pain

When a shooting pain goes down your legs and then becomes a pain in the back. Then a stabbing pain in your knee can also become a pain in the butt. Numbness in your arms can give you a pain in the neck. A pain in the chest can easily bring on a headache. The cure can be as easy as seeing a chiropractor or as difficult as surgery. A constant pain can increase depression, when a simple procedure may be all you need to feel restoration. The pills may or may not work to ease your pain. At the end of all of the torture that you are going through, it is easy to see who is a friend and who is not.

Some say that pain helps to tell yourself that you are alive, but does extensive pain for months or years make the meaning of life become lost? Pain never is the same to each one of us, but can be understood to a degree by similar patients. The pain throughout a sleepless night brings dread and exhaustion to a new day. The similarity in everyday can easily confuse the difference between a few days or a week.

As the caretaker rests his head at the end of the day, the patient's pain may return violently and it becomes another long sleepless night. Like a soldier waiting for a mission, the caretaker sleeps close by incase of trouble or help that the patient may require throughout the night. Painful screams may echo throughout the night, awaking the care giver from his slumber and within an instant be at their bedside, to give a gentle and supportive hand and other services that may be required. The anguish you feel by seeing a loved one in pain, hurts you as much as being stabbed in the heart. The grip and weight of depression can be as heavy as being tied to an anchor. Overwhelming exhaustion may come in waves in the morning as well as a deep depression causing you extreme mental pain.

Food may even become a disagreeable object to the patient. Why does the past seem to be easier during a trial, when the past trials felt just as hard at the time? An overwhelming depression comes over the patient, when the realization sets in because of losing months or years of their life, and the pain may bring many hidden emotions out of the darkness.

How much pain does someone have to be in to lose control of one self? The pain in walking, knees that collapse in daily routines, the knots in your neck and shoulders that prevent you from stretching and lifting are the pains that are supposed to say that we are human. It is truly interesting to see how fast a priority can change within a year, a week, a day or even an hour. When you are in pain the emotional twist that causes embarrassment is hard for one person to carry on their own.

A trial may end with long lasting results. The different types of therapy may all be difficult to do. But at the end it is hoped that the results will bring a world of comfort and peace; mentally, physically as well as on your outlook on life.

By going through a painful trial you grow in maturity, knowledge as well as sympathy for others. You wonder how you survived some of the hardest days that have gone by so painfully. When the patient is told that there is someone that is worse off somewhere in the world, it can be comforting to the one saying it, but to the patient it may be taken as if they are not as bad as they think they are. Can anyone go through such a trial without emotional strain? It is true there are people that have it worse, but saying it is like an old joke with an insult.

Pain can come in waves that can excel from mild to extreme making it hard for you to tell how much pain they are in. Although someone says they are fine, a mental or physical bruise can be seen, even though they do not want to show it or to talk about it.

A Life To Live

A life to live, a life to love.
Don't let your dreams fly by like a dove.
Forget how to hate.
Understand when someone is late.
Grow in talent, grow in skill.
Always remember to respect someone's will.

A life to live, a life to learn.
Don't be upset when plans take a turn.
Always be there to lend a helping hand.
Take criticism with a grain of sand.
Be there for a shoulder to cry on.
Enjoy the peace at the break of dawn.

A Life to live, a life to enjoy.
Admire the man within the boy.
Avoid fighting with each other.
Learn from your father and mother.
Smile with the innocence of a child.
Answer questions in a tone that is mild.

A life to live takes a lifetime to grow.

The Unheard Voice

I wish I had a family and to have someone to be with me and help me through the thunder storms. But I am here alone, my mother ran away and my father died long ago. I fight for what I want and I don't get along with others. I have been with other families but there has been no place for me to call home.

As the other children are adopted, I sit here watching them go. I lost my mind when they took my brother from me. What is wrong with me? Why am I here? Why can't this be a dream and to be able to wake up in a home with loving parents. I will hope and dread every day, until someone will truly accept me as a son of their own.

I have dreams for a place in my life that someone will help me to come true. Soon I will be too old to have a family of my own and will be sent to the street to learn how to live.

I can live by other peoples' standards but they haven't met me half-way yet. They don't understand how I was raised before I met them, and they always try to change me overnight.

I have tried to impress families but they don't want me. Their willingness to care is short-lived when it comes to me.

I haven't heard from my brother since his adoption. I hope he is with someone kind and that he has a peaceful start to a new life without me.

My life is uncertain at this time and no one is reaching out to me. I will once again cry myself to sleep tonight. I know it will not help anything. No one wants me and no one will hear my voice. All that I give is never enough for many parents. I will end what I am saying now.

All I wish for is for someone to love me and to give me a chance.

Looking into Love

A look into the love of a friend.
It is something that will never end.
Do you remember the walks we had?
You cheered me up when I was sad.
You stayed with me when everyone was gone.
I went for a walk you tagged along.

You only care that I feel fine.
You're not a judgmental friend of mine.
You always know when something's wrong.
You're always there when days are long.

We are as close as the shore is to the sea.
You are the best pet avoiding disapproval from me.
You always speak to me in your special way.
When I leave, I know you'll miss me all that day
Even when you make a wrong choice you know I'll love you.

Back Door to Life

I FEEL LIKE SMOKING IS THE only way that helps me with life's stress. By breathing in the smoke I feel like I am gathering my painful experiences and hardships into my chest and then, by blowing out the smoke I feel better to see the stress evaporate into the air. I know what others say about my smoking but how much does my smoking really matter to them? I smoke to relax my mind from what I still have to do. I admit that I can't go on without something to keep my hands busy and some kind of distraction from the world around me.

All those that encourage me to stop and tell me how bad smoking is, do not know the hardships that I have to go through in my life. They don't realize how hard life is without it. I can't find relief in any other way than to smoke and I hate that I am trying to hide that I am an addict but for me patches and gum are not the alternatives that I need.

To enjoy my life I need to remove my stress by seeing it vanish into thin air more than once. How can a patch on my shoulder help? I know many people that have been able to quit this way but it isn't for me. My clothes are not in the best condition from the odor of the smoke but they are fine for my job, even though strangers hold their breath and mutter when they walk by.

I remember when I was a teenager and I first started smoking. It was a big deal at my school. I started smoking to be cool and now that I am older everyone says that it will kill me. Truly my smoking alleviates the stress of the past and present and if it works for me why should I quit?

My life is peaceful but without the comfort of my smoking there is little relaxation for me in my life right now.

Crystal Bowl

Life is like a precious crystal bowl.
It is so fragile a slip could shatter, destroying it.

When you feel terrible inside,
And you feel that everyone around you knows but just doesn't care.

Knowing how it feels to lose your self-worth, self-respect and self-image,
Understanding a time when stress rules your life.

Stop and think how your family and friends would feel.
Would they be happy that they were never able to talk to you again?
That their last visit with you would have been the last one forever?

Think about all the lives you have changed in the past,
And also the happiness that you have given to others.

Always think about others before you make your decision.
A wrong decision can bring a world of pain to others.

It is far better for the crystal bowl to collect dust,
Than to allow it to shatter.

Like An Echo

Like an echo,
I hear your voice behind me.
But like a dream, you're gone.
My hearts sinks, my joy fades.

I have always known that it was our choice.
As the sun turns into the moon, and rain turns to snow.
I blow the dust off the frames, while waiting to see you again.
As a cavern, you are only an echo.

Like a memory, you are transparent.
I have fought for us, but now it is time to put down my sword,
And rest my weary body and bruised muscles.
Like an echo, no one responds to my call.

Like the wind, you seem to talk to me.
But you are miles away, beyond the sea
We said nothing would pull us apart.
Now our words are echoes, in a darkened canyon.

Dividing from the Shattered

GRIEF TO HIDE FROM AND pain to cry out in are caused by the fights that are heard from the bedroom above and creates a tortuous life that makes striding away from it a brighter decision. While wandering, lost in the darkness of confusion, you must always keep walking strong, as the crumbling supports crack and erode in the building of the marriage. Unsure of what path to take you turn to friends for help. Some may then avoid you, some may try to destroy and attack you, but many will be there to help and support you throughout the turbulence of reality.

During the end of a loveless marriage the two lives and emotions will never be the same again. As a bowl of hot water the emotions for each other have become cold over time. The circuit of communication seems to have been cut as if by a pair of wire cutters. At times venomous lies may be fired in order to destroy each other's charter, and to show how wise and kind they are out of arrogance.

There is much love, dedication, trust and respect lost throughout years of a troubled married life. What problems can one person go through that a couple can't travel through together? Although there is a divorce out of anger and hurt there may still be some feelings left, even though they may not be mutual. Be sure that all children that have been subjected to this way of life

know that it is NOT THEIR FAULT and that they don't claim
the burden of guilt for their own.

Anger and friction grow from within as if they were fires
under a kettle of water. As the relationship ends, lines are drawn
in the sand and fights start between ownership of personal objects.
Friends may even lose their respect for you because your marriage
has failed. The shallowness from some friends can be instant or
can grow over time. With most divorces commutation wires are
cut and sometimes for no good reason.

Criticism comes from family and friends who give their
personal point of view. What pushes people farther apart
than broken communication? The blameless often feel guilty
and usually the ones that changed are the ones that deny any
responsibility. The cold in their heart is like a winter's night of
wildly blowing snow. It is similar to that of the friction between
the two families that shifts like the eroding plates in the earth.

The child usually finds more comfort from one parent than
the other one. Why does one parent often blame the other for the
destruction of the love between parent and child?

The strength of your heart is what will pull you through.

Like a Butterfly

Like a butterfly your wings show your colors.
Your determination is shown in the way you fly into turbulent winds.
You are afraid to be looked upon and judged with wrath.
You have no choice but to spread your wings and show yourself or you will never be happy.

You will never get to where you want to be in your life with hesitation.
Don't be afraid to open your wings. Even moths open their wings to the world.
The fragility in your wings is what makes you afraid to stand when everyone else is sitting.
When you walk you walk close to the ground, with your wings closed.

You try to hide yourself by covering your bright colors with your dull side.
As you continue to shelter your talents, you will forget how to fly.
Your wings show your colors like a butterfly.

Adult before Age

LOOKED DOWN UPON FOR THE child you have.

Shunned for your age and the history of your actions.

Abortions out of fear for the responsibility and the time that you don't have.

Your boyfriend, the one that said, "Nothing will make us part." Has now gone and is with someone new. Giving up school activities, sleep, money and your plans for the future have vanished. You may feel lost, deep in depression and desperation. Lost time, money and learning create a sadness of dependence and at times defiance. You are ashamed to tell your parents and become sick with fear of how they will take the news. When the time is right you will look to your parents for their supportive hands, forgiveness, love and comfort. Some parents raise their hands in a way of barricading, while others open doors and arms with kindness.

The choices made in the present will change the future that we may want. An abortion may be faster but your conscience cannot be outrun nor can it be hidden from. Guilt hits hard and sleep may be lost on an active mind. Thoughts of being worthless come as if they were thrown into the river of your sole. Self-worth shatters a heavy heart, and your conscience can belittle you from within.

That one night will give you over eighteen years of caring which is the same care that you required from birth. It may be hard but the years will go fast, although at the time it seems to drag on. Choices come with a costly price no matter how small an action.

Hopelessness is in your eyes, your ex-boyfriend is on your mind and you wish that the time you had had with him would have pulled you closer together.

Now looking into the mirror you see yourself as a parent and nothing looks the same and yet there is a familiarity. The unfinished knowledge of becoming a parent in a world of the unforgiving will never have a path that has a railing to hold onto. Your self-consciousness will be hurt, and your dreams may be extinguished with the new plans for the unborn. Your pride and love will be something like you have ever experienced before. All that you thought and imagined for the caring of a child, cannot be imagined, it will be a complete and total reality.

An experience that takes a lifetime to learn is the hardest and most amazing thing that will change your mind, life, and its teachings.

Whether you have the child or have an abortion your feelings will forever be imbedded in your heart and mind in one way or another.

Don't beat yourself down for your past but step forward with what you have done and grow stronger with your acceptances.

Thinking Back

WHEN I LOOK AT MY life and I see all that I have accomplished, I smile at how small my failed goals are and how my view of life has changed. All the plans that had to be rearranged and how life went on no matter how large the problems were. Then I think of how my life would have been, if certain problems would have never happened, and who I would have been today. When my past returns to the present or when the past becomes the topic, I can't believe how far I have traveled to reach here. I have met many people, some became close friends, some became enemies, and others have gone their separate ways.

I sometimes wonder what happened to my old friends from school. Although the years drag by my memories are as far away as if it were yesterday, and future plans have a way of having to wait longer than normal. Soon the past will turn into dusts and the memories of a previous time into a stale must.

Why do we remember all that went wrong in our own life but often seem to forget the enjoyment that comes with life? If life gets you down and you can't seem to get back onto your feet always smile even if it is for no reason. No matter how you live life it always seems to pass by peacefully like a sailboat or as a fast jet. The past is a mystery of forgotten recollections. Regret and pain takes over if you hold it close to your heart.

I made mistakes and I've taken my punishment. I hung my head as I walked the path that I have made for myself. The lives that I have hurt by my mistakes and actions have lost some peoples respect for me.

I have learned since then, that you can let go, and everything will and can be fine. The guilt will forever be there but the facts are, that time heals all wounds as well as the pain from within. The life I have had and remember I now see in others that I meet.

I wish I had learned more at school because when I look at where I am now I become frustrated but I smile at the goals I had as a child. Thinking back I can't believe how small my dreams were as to what they are now. I wish that I had finished all that I started.

In retrospect to others in my past I have now seen and understand most of what my friends tried to tell me. I am not the same person that I was thirty years ago but then neither is the world.

Is everything that I have gone through only to become memories, to become forgotten when I get older?

Quaking under pressure.

Y OU HAVE THE SINKING FEELING of your heart that is pounding in your chest because of the family crisis.

You are breaking down from the school work that is landing on your desk.

You have taken the attacks from school personally and also the family arguments to heart.

All is growing upon your own ghosts and accumulating the hurtful voices to weave a dark sweater of failures.

The times you have given into what you never wanted to do.

The pressure you feel to be better than you are for your parents, then finding out that it was all out of reach.

You are unable to move on from a death of a family member or a friend.

Feeling as if you had buried your heart six feet deep alongside of them.

You are fighting with the politics of your job and the back stabbing from your best friend at school and nights of dwelling on your actions, when you should be sleeping.

Times when the past looked better than the future of the upcoming week.

It is your conscience that doesn't let you forgive yourself by tearing you apart from within. Looking back on other's betrayal angers you, during your hurtful depression. How is it that your stress grew into something more than an emotion?

You have become handicapped, unable to walk as far as you once did. Losing your voice and or suffering from amnesia also may happen, all because of the environment that you are living in. Stress is like a cancer of the mind that we all have, and yet it affects everyone differently.

Finding yourself alone, and wanting others to know how you feel, and yet not wanting to explain to them why you have become troubled. You feel you deserve a treat but are depressed about how you look in the mirror.

There were days that leaving your room and going outside was a mistake. Stress is something that we can't avoid and the drama is like that of a cat after a mouse.

Those that come to attack you are like shadows in a dense forest waiting to ambush you. Your friends are like a crew on a ship willing to help you when you are stranded in the water. The sharks are always there but the crew is also there to help you with your stress. How much stress does it take to make your world crumble around you?

How can we run our own life smoothly when drama is always on our door step? When the light is too bright for your eyes turn to your friends to help bring you up off of your knees, to help you stand, and to rise against the childish mocking's that you receive from others. Your true friends will still think you are great, even after you have fallen. You may ask why this is happening to you now? But when the time comes, and all is placed in a so called box in the back, you will realize how strong you really are. The future will look bright even though the past is a broken road of broken friendships and crushed dreams.

Whatever happens or happened in your life must be put into the past for you to be able to grow from it. You don't see yourself the way your friends see you. All of what you knew about your life is now gone and your outlook has become like an old picture without clarity or brightness. To know who is a friend or a foe, look at those that are trying to talk you through the stressful times.

The mind is what keeps everything in tact but the chaos in your mind is what breaks apart the physical and mental gears.

Dream of the Famous

I UNEXPECTEDLY CAUGHT A GLIMPSE OF you in a television commercial. My heart came to a dead stop in shock and surprise and I wondered what it would be like to be next to you. Then I tell myself that I wouldn't be happy with that imaginary lifestyle although I continue to dream of it. I become depressed when standing in a crowd of thousands or perhaps millions of people who have the same wants as I have. As you become more famous I realize that I should be happy and comfortable in my own life because not every single dream or want happens in reality. As I watch you on the television screen, it looks like you have it all. Although I have dreamed in spending some time with you, reality would have run me over if I had stopped to look. Apart from the denial and acceptance of my life, I now see how my neutral life is rolled out in front of me as if it were a carpet.

When you look out and see all of your fans, I'll be in the far corner smiling in admiration and in hope that someday I too will be noticed by you. There have been days where I have imagined us together, but then I remember where I came from, and that I'm not going anywhere since I can't sing, act, or even be a good comedian.

Every once in a while I ask myself what kind of a life would I have, forever getting married and divorced, being slandered by many magazines and being chased by fans and the paparazzi must be frustrating. Your smallest actions are caught on every phone and camera, and the stress of being judged for the clothes you wear and the drugs that everyone is pressured to partake in.

Truly there is a good reason why I am nobody and you have become so successful. I will always admire you for what you have done with your life. I am not the type to travel from hotel to hotel and country after country. Your love is for your fans; your kindness is for your family and the ones you work with. I am only an ant in a colony of thousands.

Why does a fake reality always seam brighter than what we have right now? Even if our imaginations were real we still would not be happy. True happiness will only come by having a peaceful mind, not by all of the longing desires that we want. What we want and what we need are always mixed and confusing but when we lose everything we receive new eyes, and see the world from a different perspective, one that we have never seen before.

The day I look intently into the mirror and see myself for who I really am, in some ways will be the day I dread the most. Why is it that I am not where I wanted to be in this life? My life is calm and stress free, but there seems to be some sort of an imaginary want which is not a part of reality.

A Living Loss

The sorrow.

   The grief.

      The pain.

         The warped mental stability.

As a pallbearer I stood behind the hearse ready to carry my loved one's casket into the church. During the viewing many feelings came out. Some pain, some sorrow, a little bit of jealously, anger and a vivid vibe was coming off of the disrespected outcasts of the family. Slowly the denial that he was gone became overwhelmingly painful, followed by an acceptance that he had died.

The outcasts stood alone in a corner, being troubled by their own sorrow and being supported by their own thoughts as the widow vanished into the mass of grieving people supporting her.

We somberly walked into the chapel. The redwood casket was at the front, with a red and golden casket spray on top of it, along with two smiling photos of him. As we sat down, the minister walked up to the microphone, and started the funeral service. Tears seemed to flow like rain drops, as his sister did the eulogy.

The heartache came in loud sniffles of sadness, as I looked around to see dozens of tissues being passed around to wipe their eyes and to blow their noses. As they praised the man they thought they knew, I looked around the room at the tearful faces to see who believed that he had been a saint. I knew a different kind of a man than they spoke of, because of the turmoil that he had put me through, I somberly cried in longing for the friendship that they spoke of.

Then as the organ played it was time to carry my uncle back out of the chapel. As I lifted the cold brass handle, the only thing that went through my mind was "IT IS OVER." But seeing their sadness, my heart ached for them. I became angry with myself for having a heavy heart that sank to the bottom of the ocean for the family, and not feeling bad that he was gone.

After we carefully placed the casket in the hearse I turned around to see his five year old son, full of tears, give a small wave with his little hand from the protection of his mother's arms. He then wrapped her in a hug, as the hearse slowly and silently drove away.

Forest Voices

THE DRY LEAVES FELL GENTLY to the ground and their murmurings were overheard in the voice of the wind. The remaining few leaves dangled from the tree limbs. A chickadee nestled on a bare branch before chirping to the wind and a squirrel dashed across the dead leaves on the beaten dirt path on its hunt for food. My deep visible breaths drifted through the crisp October air. A whisper of a memory from my grandfather seemed to echo through the rustle of the remaining dry leaves that hung on the bare trees.

Within the coming weeks snow and frost will cover all the paths and all will become a scenery of winter brightness. The overhead sun now brightens the path ahead which in summer was always covered in shade. The silence that hung in the air was broken only by the leaves crumbling underfoot, a few small animals preparing for winter and my slightly heavy breathing.

As I look at my surroundings and all the trees around me, I continued on with my rejuvenating walk down the path, which led me back to the gray and brown building.

My truck came into view in the parking lot as well as a few other vehicles from other families that had come to see the Forest Reserve. I looked at my watch and saw that it was a quarter after twelve and a family was gathering around their car getting ready to leave this peaceful facility. Thoughtfully I smiled at the chattering crowd as I climbed into my rusting blue truck and began surveying the area for a fast food restaurant parking lot that wasn't completely congested with vehicles.

A Darkness Without Much Light

I HAVE FOUGHT TO KEEP MYSELF healthy and I have kept away from unhealthy foods, eating mostly everything that is organic.

It was a heartbreaking day at the hospital when the doctor broke the news to me and my family. That day it felt like the hospital had fallen on me and my life had begun a count down. I wish I could go back in time before being taken over by cancer. Every day I felt uncertain whether I was going survive or not. The chemotherapy was scheduled and I wondered daily what will happen to my family. I know that my children will grow up and become fine young adults, but I fear that I will not be there for them, to help them through life.

What forces me to continue on, is not only the fear of dying but the fear of not knowing how my family will handle my absence. My devastating news shot dread through everyone that I know like venom, spiraling out of control. I am afraid of my absence from my family more than the fear of death. All that I have planned has come to an end, but I will never give up on life. I will never let all that my mate and children have done for me go in vain, because I will conquer what I have and be there for my family.

I am grieved when I hear what other people are going through, and I sympathize with the children that have such painful burdens to carry on their shoulders.

The young when stricken, seem to have bright dreams and goals in spite of the cancer and seem to be unafraid of the uneven balance of their life. As they lie in bed they show their strength in how they support their parents though the heart wrenching mental and physical pain of cancer. I see the sympathy in people's eyes as they look into the room as they walk by.

The candle that lights the path that I walk on does not show the end of the slightly gusty tunnel that I travel in alone. I may be a victim but I won't be one that will lose easily. I become depressed and do wish it were all to end by sunrise, but I cannot abandon those that have given me everything. I will not let their faith in me be in vain. My family has said that we can beat this and they are the ones that help me and prevent me from giving up.

I will refuse to let the cancer beat me. As long as my family doesn't give up I will forever fight to be beside them.

When you have nothing to live for, you live for others.

Seven Bills

Someone put 7 bills on a clear glass table.
A sudden blast of hot air blew the first one.
A twenty fell onto the floor under a chair.
The second one was crumpled into a ball.
The third was an old Canadian dollar bill.
The forth, a fifty, was still in the center of the table.
The fifth had a fold in the middle.
The sixth was a five still face up on the table.
When I looked again the seventh one, a hundred,
Had disappeared from the table.
Leaving me to wonder where did it go.

Dream of Another Culture

Who I am and who I want to be are as far apart as an attic is from a basement.
My clothes are tattered and torn from use.
I feel distressed and lonely.
My hair could use a trim.
Eating at soup kitchens morning, noon and night.
Sitting on the curb, rethinking my life.
People walk by, avoiding my plea.
I look down in shame seeing my ex-wife.

From within this is who I dream to be.
Wearing soft clothes with bright colors.
Unafraid of the chance of being robbed.
Being carefree and outgoing.
Looked up to by others.
I'm on the cover of every magazine.
I have the perfect life that I have always wanted.
I smile as I drive my expensive car towards the sunset.

Riddle #1

I disappear as fast as the sun in the winter.

Like trust I take a long time to gain.

Like lightning I can disappear in a flash.

Like a drug, I am hard to stop.

I can't be stopped, just like an immune virus.

I am unstoppable and you can't live without me.

What am I?

Riddle #2

I am a feeling and an action.

People consider me blind at times.

Some people don't know they even have me.

I am a gift that can be sent many ways.

People have done and said many things in my name.

What am I?

Riddle #3

People lose their mind over me.

I come like a tornado.

If they throw me at someone, they usually get sucked in as well.

After I do my job, they don't realize how much they have had to pay.

My price is mental, financial and the respect of your name.

Like a cold hearted killer,

I show no mercy.

What Am I?

Riddle #4

I am an opportunity.

Like makeup, I can change a person's personality.

People who can't handle me become self-righteous and undermining.

If abused for too long, I retaliate by vanishing, and watch you sink like a rock in the river of reality

I hear your cries of self-pity but I know that you did this to yourself.

What am I?

Riddle #5

Like music I can seem calm or fierce.

People should fear me, but the ignorant stand in front of me mockingly.

The power and speed I have, is spread across me.

At my home I am as fast as a jet but as I climb higher, I slowly become tired and return home with whatever I can carry.

What am I?

Answers to riddles on page 97

Wanting to lose

I AM ASHAMED AND EMBARRASSED WITH the way I look in the mirror. I am always avoiding attention by standing in the back and wearing loose and dark clothes to hide myself. Being afraid of attracting attention, I avoid tying my shoes in the school hallway and eating in public. I skip meals to lose more weight and worry what others will say if I indulge in eating greasy foods or those foods that the professionals say are unhealthy. The quiet table in the corner of the cafeteria is my place to hide from everyone. I feel like everyone is staring at me and judging me by my weight. I hate the weight that I have on my waist, face, stomach, and legs. Wishing to look like the person on the magazine cover I cry every night for who I have become. Wanting to hide my body, I keep to myself. I lie to avoid having to go to pool parties. I always keep my clothes clean and spotless to avoid comments about being a slob and lazy in people's eyes. When friends invite me to go to restaurants, I turn them down because I know that someone will comment on what I am eating.

I have tried almost every diet and strategy, starting with high hopes and excitement which then turns into a little success and ends with a heavy heart. I ask and wonder, "Why me? Why is it that all I do is never good enough?" I also wonder "How can I change to who I want to be?" Even the model's body, that I wish

I had, hates what she sees in the mirror, and is fighting to lose more weight. Like the model, I am fighting to get rid of what I see, because I think that is what others see. I avoid eating around other people and only eat behind closed doors, in the comfort of my home. Behind closed doors is where I can relax and don't have to put on a show, by eating something that makes me feel like everyone else. Then I don't have to eat what pleases others because they are not there to joke about my eating.

I work harder than my body will allow, my legs are wrecked and I am unable to walk as I did before. My knees are worm and sore and it hurts to walk, although I try to hide it. I walk with a limp.

I am embarrassed when I go shopping because I don't fit into the averaged sized clothes. The employees ignore or belittle me cruelly, when I am looking around in their store.

I am never given credit for what I have done in the past or for the weight I have lost. This is why I never eat in public places. I am saddened for how I look and I have lost all hope.

I can't understand how others have been able to lose so much in such a little amount of time, and it frustrates me that I can't do the same. I just don't know what to do anymore and after every diet I try to accept that I will be fat for the rest of my life. Telling myself that I am like this crushes me, because even with all my determination, my weight is still out of my control.

I could tell you anything about any diet that I have tried and everything has been engraved into my mind. I admire the people on the TV that have lost all the weight they wanted to. What makes me feel so horrible is not to be able to lose the weight that others have done so easily.

I never look at photo albums because they only depress me because in the pictures I see what I looked like before and what I look like now. I have never been happy with who I am and those that are my true friends understand how I feel. If you look through my home you won't see many pictures of me.

Even when all hope is gone and you are exhausted from fighting with your weight and close to crying, remember that a new dawn brings a refreshing start to a new day.

Understanding Life Through a Bottle

Staring blankly into the air, in the kitchen
Depression creeps over me, as if it were a flannelette blanket.
My life has passed me by, as I sat doing nothing for my future,
While someone else was playing with my family.

Time has passed by so quickly, I barely saw my daughter mature.
Sorrowed by the loneliness, I longingly glance at the phone.
Afraid to make an attempt to call, I wonder how to overcome this fear.
Confused, I quickly become afraid of righting the wrongs that I have done.

Wishing the phone would ring, I begin to realize how forgotten I am to my family.
How my daughter and I have drifted apart.
She is probably happier with her new family without me in it, I reminded myself.
Whatever I have done has never been good enough for her.

Even if I did phone, what was there I could say or do to change the past?

I live alone in deafening silence surrounded only by my memories.

I sit here dwelling on my life because it seems brighter from within the bottle.

Afraid to open up, I become more depressed as I take another bottle and another drink.

Old Store

A STORE SILENT AND DYING HAS seen many events over the years, from witnessing fires, heat, drought and from being rescued from floods and many months of heavy snowfall. He now stands empty, sad, and depressed. Day after day standing alone through the driving rain remembering when his owner would light the fireplace in the back of the building. The windows have now turned yellow from crying himself to sleep night after night.

The old store befriends the trapped flies between the tear stained windows for friendship since everyone abandoned him long ago. He says one final farewell before shifting his weight onto another beam of his structural system as he then begins cracking unknowingly. He then leans more on his weaker side and screams in sudden pain and surprise as the pressure cracks the wooden supports. Unsteadily he uselessly tries to grab his footing as he collapses onto his side, shattering widows and bending the metal shelves that are within him.

He then takes one final breath before completely relaxing because there is nothing left to do but to stare at the sun rising in the east.

The Words Before Goodbye

Since when did we exchange farewell for see ya.
I never even introduced you to my ma 'n pa.
You walked into the cab, letting me stand in the rain.
You were my support, my strength my cane.
I thought I lost all of my life.
That I was too weak for all of the strife.

What happened to us?
I tried to hold on.
But all has crumbled with rust.
Why have we lost the trust?
Even the canary in the kitchen has grown quiet.
I never meant what I said in that riot.

You walked into the cab letting me stand in the rain.
You were my support, my strength, my cane.
I thought I lost all of my life.
That I was too weak for all of the strife.

Our love has turned to dust in the wind.
I wish I could have asked you to stay.
But the ticket was in your pocket.
Our past is now on my mind.
I wish our talks were not on line.

I wish I could tell you those three words again.
I Love You.

A Realization of Reality

How do other people's lives affect your life? Why do some strangers seem kinder than a close friend? Reality plays around with our lives as if playing with spinning tops, watching us stumble and fall under trouble and trials. Life takes and throws troublesome trials in front of our feet. It is like misstepping on a flight of stairs. Like climbing a mountain, the rocky ground is difficult all the way to the summit of peace and relaxation. Maturity has a chance to grow through the blind immaturity of their self-respect and self-worth. You can never really tell how hard life is until it becomes harder. Life is a teacher that never hands out homework but always gives a surprise test that we haven't prepared for.

Why don't some fears become trials while others that we haven't considered become worse than what we dreaded? We must keep waking and occasionally look back at the footprints that we had left behind. If you have confidence, nothing can stop you from a dream or a plan. Not all plans will go the way we want them to go but all goals can be accomplished with extreme dedication and a set heart. There are people around the world that try to live an easy life, not wanting to learn, unwilling to grow, and lost in a reality of their own.

Truly the more you know about everything around you, the more it seems to be like the dark part of a stone. Even a friendly smile to a stranger brings a glimmer of light, like a child's hope and innocence. Always try to avoid the whip of wrath and the knife that portrays its glimmer of gold and power, for sooner or later it will stab you in the back. Not one person has had an easy or free pass through life.

This world and life is full of contradictions, confusion and grief no matter how old you become. It is possible to overcome life's problems if you set your mind to it. If life came with an instruction manual it would make as much sense as a complex foreign language. The only answer to life is to move on and to tackle the future no matter how uncertain the future is, and always do your best to succeed through the strife of life.

Life is unfair and will always be unfair and it is up to you to fight for what you want and to be strong in you decisions and actions. No one else will stand up for you and it is up to you to do a good job. If life was easy, pride and satisfaction would be earned by doing nothing and a person's life would not be interesting and their life's stories would not be worth reading.

Life is a never ending reality that will continue long after the end of the last chapter of your life has been written. Although life turns like the tide it does become peaceful and times of enjoyment do come.

No matter how hard life gets, it will never be harder than what you can handle.

Once a Friend . . . Now an Enemy

Read my lips, understand what I say.
You try to hurt me, behind my back, every day.
Stop spreading your lies.
I'm not living in fury, just in exasperated sighs.

Live your own life, in anger or in spite.
I now realize what you are really like.
Once a friend, now an enemy.
Remember at school and at the academy?
Learning together, we laughed as close friends.
I wonder what happened, to make it all end.

I walk into the room, to see your unwelcome stare.
You act as if, I am not really there.
Why do you rebuke me?
It came so suddenly, I still can't see.
The room becomes quiet, when I'm present.
Even through your coldness, I try to act pleasant.

Perhaps I don't understand your reasons, but do I understand mine.
Never again will I turn to you to cry, I will be fine!

My life has not lost meaning without you.
I can only hope that you can find peace too.

The only question I have is "Why do you hate so?"

Black and Blue to the Soul

Beaten, swollen and attacked personally and openly.

The anonymous insults on-line,

The attacks that lead children into quitting the game of life early,

The believers that die from the malicious and cruel words at school,

The easily preventable situations that happen next,

A Life of happiness that many of the young have forgotten,

Your personality becomes a stranger to yourself.

Your own beaten self becomes unnoticeable even to your reflection in the mirror.

The shove on school grounds,

The personal tease everyone is snickering about.

"WORTHLESS" AND "BETTER OFF DEAD," are knives to your heart, self-esteem and drive. Their mental played threats keep you silent in fear. You try to avoid the troublesome group that follows you tauntingly and picks on the nerves that keep you steady headed. As hatred builds up and grows within you, it is like a balloon that can burst suddenly without any signs.

When a weapon is carried onto the school grounds it is often from uncontrollable anger of revenge that exceeds the fear of the consequences.

Although the first hand comes forward in defense, whether it was for verbal mocking, mind gaming or for a comeback swing, the victim is somehow always the one to pay the guilty culprits price.

Pressure to fit in becomes like a fight for a first class ticket that goes against your own character, friends, your family, conscience and the up-bringing that you have had. You are teased for a point of view that you have had all your life. The words of compassion and respect are forgotten by the heartless and thoughtless. The cruelty from others comes from frustration, pain from the past, or the fear of losing control.

Afraid to speak what's on your mind, some people find alternatives for dealing with the pain. Some rise up against the terrorist, some turn to a parent, while others live with it, but unfortunately some will never recover. The scarred and beaten never forget what they have gone through while the bullies have forgotten their past many years ago. The open scars may heal with time or with help, which many at first feel is useless or unneeded and should be dealt with from within.

The character building that everyone talks about is an excuse given for a growing mind to be abused and degraded. It is truly an unfortunate action that must be stopped at all possible cost. Yet it is something that cannot be stopped but only slightly prevented to the physical sight.

Zero tolerance is pushed for physical bullying, but where does it take a stand when the bulling comes by destructive gossip or on-line? Why does a victim get punished when they are pushed past their breaking point and the perpetrator is punished with no more than a slap on their wrist?

Not only students but also judgmental teachers may find you less worthy and lower their expectations of you. Some teachers lecture you in front of the class, lowering your grades below the rightful grade mark, as well as criticizing you for the way you answered a question. What are you to do when a teacher dislikes you for who you are?

Not all teachers push you down but many pull you up from the ground in your class. They are dedicated to hold you up because they see more in you than you may see in yourself.

Teachers are like medication, with the right teacher you can find the cure for any trouble you are having.

A Past Wished to Be Forgotten

I LIVE WITH MY PAST EVERY night. I have been on the front of newspapers and on television. I have learned and spent my time trying to live past my mistakes but they have become viral to live on forever. I was young and didn't know better, but some say that it is no excuse. Even now that I am out of prison and have paid the price some people have not forgiven me.

Unable to find a job, I live with my older brother. Everyone that has met me without knowing of my background likes me, but when they learn about my past, they watch me suspiciously. Truly, although I have done everything to be forgiven, I have lost some of their respect forever. Those that are self-righteous see me as someone that doesn't deserve a second chance. I am fighting for what I want in life but there is no end to the backstops and tailspins. I have learned much since then and yet you can't accept that I made a costly mistake that has hurt many people. Therefore you feel that I cannot change. When I ask what others would have done, the answer always is, that they would have acted differently.

I can't sleep at night because my conscience and thoughts keep me awake when I lay my head down. No one knows how hard I have damaged myself with my own thoughts. I hold back tears of anger and hurt because of my foolish and irresponsible actions in my past. I always seem to be telling myself how stupid I was to do what I did. The day I went to prison was the day I lost almost everyone around me. My girlfriend dumped me, my parents now avoid the phone when I call them, and my friends scatter when I approach.

I have lost my life opportunities while my buddy cares little about what we did and to this day I have still accepted his part of the blame for what happened and I haven't seen him since the trial.

You still feel that you have the right to say that I am worth nothing, not even a second look. I wish I could go back in time and change who I was then to the person I am now. I was an immature punk making my own rules rather than following other people's advice and ignoring the help they desperately tried to give me. I am ashamed to talk to my parents now and regret what I have done in the past. Now I am labeled as a convict. My heart is heavy with a guilty conscience and with my own accusations.

Punishment tells you right from wrong but a reward teaches you why to do right.

Judged by the Judgmental Pride

DEGRADED BY MY LOOKS, I am judged for what I wear. Because I wear dark clothes I am seen as untrustworthy and rebellious without even saying a word. You think that because someone wears dark eyeliner it makes them beneath you. My spiked bag and chained jacket show only who I am on the outside not from within. How can you judge me for wearing black when the widow at the funeral and those that are overweight wear dark to shadow themselves from others.

You judgmentally stare mindlessly at my nose and lip piercings as if distracted by a glimmer of light. Your superficial pride shows in the look in your eyes and your childish actions. I always feel your eyes on me, I hear your silent remarks, and I can see the reactions on your face. How can you treat me like this when all I do is speak respectfully? I may wear dark clothes but your darkness is in your cold judgmental heart hidden under white and colorfully decorated clothes. Although I am dressed differently, why can't you treat me the same?

I am not a freak, nor a person that should be feared. This is MY LIFE and there is no reason to change it to go with your expectations. If I were to change it would be for me not for your so-called concern for me. How can you expect me to be who I am and do what you tell me to do at the same time? If I am fine with myself, why can't you be?

I may be rebelling against my unreasonable parents but they don't care about me. Their religion and their friends come first. I have tried everything and been respectful but there is nothing you do except stare at me and treat me differently. My tattoos only show who I am, what I feel and what I have been through. But those that look down on me for what I have done with my life, don't see what I have gone through in my personal life.

You don't know me and yet when I leave I know you shake your head in disapproval and when I walk by you turn and look back at me. Who are you to decide my fate through your stereotype decisions and shortsightedness? Places find what I wear unacceptable and the employers look the other way.

I have changed what I was like because I could not compete with my brother's accomplishments and the respect he was given so I have become someone different from what he portrays himself to be. There is no reason for the way you act, so why do you act the way you do? Those that are prejudice call me rebellious and those that are strong in their religious beliefs call me a demon worshiper. You may not have said it to my face, but it is still clear to me what you think by the way you look at me. How fair is it for you to turn and point and to break me down, when I did nothing to you?

There is more to people than what they wear but clothes are a definition as to who you are.

Tattoos are an explanation of one's personal life and emotions.

Spinning in Determination

Determination~Dedication~Education~Enthusiasm~
Will~Passion~Love.

These are the descriptions in conquering a fight to be the best. A fight to the top takes long hours and a love for the work at hand. You want the respect of others for a job well done, as well as having satisfaction in ourselves for a grand performance. Whatever your passion is, always be strong and enthusiastic in what you do. The strongest will be seen in a crowd of thousands and letting yourself stand tall in a crowd will allow you to be seen for who you are. Fight whatever is in the way for what you want. It is true that the harder you work the harder you can fall, but take that risk and prove that you are unstoppable. As a fight to be better becomes a fight for the best, don't become blind with self-confidence for it can be your victor or it can lead to your own downfall. Not much has been accomplished without hard work or some type of influence. Fighting for what you want makes the reward greater and the pride in what you are doing stronger. Whatever you do, do it with all your might. Then whatever the outcome take pride in what you have accomplished.

As the minutes turn into hours, few things can stop a dream, a goal, or a plan. Discouragement comes with time and over time plans may turn into rubble for lack of dedication or having a change of plans. Don't stop short before succeeding or you will forever regret what you could have done. Don't let yourself lose interest in your passion. The power of will and the power of want makes the difference between doing something in a moment or in a year as strength is pulled out of your heart and the passionate part of your mind. Passion is something that should not be discouraged or dismissed by anyone. What people want you to do will never be as good as what you love to do most. Nothing can prevent you from succeeding with your dreams if you don't let it. The urging desire from within can be the driving force that leads to a masterpiece which you have created, because an unfinished project is worse than a project that hasn't been started.

I have not accomplished all of what I wanted in life yet, so I will continue to fight against all the odds to accomplish my unfinished goals that others say are unrealistic. The things that I said I would do, I have done and much more, far beyond what I dreamed I would be able to do.

My pride is reflected in the finished result of a job well done.

Between the Scars

I REMEMBER THE TIME WHEN IT was only me, that was before my brother was born. I was my parent's only child and their pride and joy. Now my parents look the other way when I approach, I am always the last person to be introduced, and the first person looked at when something goes wrong. My brother feels the conflict between our parents and me. I am jealous because of the way they treat him, but I know there is nothing more that I can do to gain their respect. When my brother sees what is happening, I wish I did not see the pain in his eyes. He hates how I am treated but loves the attention and the expensive gifts he receives, while I receive cheap gifts.

Our parent's attention is focused on their friends and on my brother, and I am not given credit for what I do. I am not going to give up on my brother because he is always there when I need him the most. Especially the times when I was mad, depressed, or in tears, he always made me smile. I am truly jealous of him because he is treated better than I am. He always gets what he wants and I can't even get my name written on a birthday cake.

I feel like most of my life has been a mistake. I am a person that is always being compared to others as never being good enough. I know that they are only trying to inspire me but does it always have to be a contest with my life. Once our parents finally see me as a part of the family, I will be at peace with myself. I hate that my little brother is always given a clean slate and they remember everything that I have done wrong in the past. They even bring up the childish things which I did when I was nine and I am also the one who is not allowed to go to parties.

Whenever I disagree with our parents, I am disciplined and become a disappointment in their eyes. My brother only gets a slap on the wrist and then forgiveness. I am asked to do the chores around the house and am also more restricted as to where I can go with my friends. A hopeless shadow behind my brother is all that I am to our parents. I feel betrayed and that is why I rarely talk to our parents and turn to my friends concerning everything that is happening in my life.

Looking at my life there are some things to be thankful for. I was proud to be able to watch my little brother from the sidelines as he grew up.

Living in an overshadowed life, I am learning how to live contently.

Someday I will find the sun and have my own day at the beach.

SCHOOL
Child to student
Student to teacher
Understanding comes willingly
Like from a preacher.

STORY
Sentence into paragraph
Paragraph into story
Words from life
Thank you and sorry.

HOW TO GROW
Growing through life
Growing though love
Hitting the bumps of life
Fight your fears, to grow above.

CHILD
Caring causes love
Happiness causes a smile
Innocence causes peace
Life causes learning
Dependence is the first step for a CHILD

LIFE
Let your care for others become balanced with the care for yourself.
If there is a river obstructing your path, let the help of a friend make it passable
Fight to make your dreams and plans to become possible
Everything can be learned from, if you pay attention to **LIFE**'s surroundings.

A Fading Recollection

I WALK INTO OUR COMFORTABLE LIVING room to see my father sitting there on his rocking chair, reading the daily newspaper for the eighth time, as I begin preparing supper in the kitchen. Those who only see us sometimes don't see the whole story but our friends see it as a life of drama and a life of hardship. It is the only life that I know. My true friends come to help me every couple of days with keeping the house clean and making meals. It is hard to look after my father but even harder to think of the guilty and helpless feelings that I would have by taking him to a nursing home. When making decisions, I am often stuck at a fork in the road trying to do the right thing.

It pains me to see him wandering around lost at home or when he stands in a doorway with a blank expression on his face, unsure of what to do. Our fights are never easy throughout the day because of his confusion and exhaustion. Places and people at times have become a darkened betrayal to his mind. His life is like a blank piece of paper and his health has taken away any future plans of traveling. He always sits in his rocking chair and at times crying for all that he has lost. He is now beginning to lose his voice for words.

It is the pain of the knowing what will happen in the future, and the pain of what we are going through right now. All I can do is to continue helping him the way he helped me in the past and I know that I will be with him to the end.

He denies his age and it is a continuous fight with me about his independence. Fearing that my father will leave in the dead of night causes many sleepless nights for me. Every few hours he goes to the kitchen wanting to wash dishes, to watch television in the living room, or wanting to go out for a late night walk.

I fear the day that I snap and say something that I will forever regret. I hold his hand and make a promise to myself, that I will never betray him or leave him where I am not able to help him. I have seen people give up and leave their parents in nursing homes to live out the rest of their lives alone.

No one understands why I don't give up and place him in a home. It aches to see him walk around the house trying to find a blanket or sweater which is hanging on a kitchen chair in plain sight.

Losing the past is similar to losing your life, for there is not much left but to start again if possible.

The Titan Warriors

We have conquered all that was not possible.
We have traveled the distance where others have wandered off long ago.

We have fought to be noticed and recognized.
We have stood through the hail storms without anyone handing us a hand for support.

Although we have been hit by lightning and stones, our backs have not given in to the pain.
We are walking beyond the worn soles of our shoes.

Shaking off the snow and dirt, we have outlasted the blinding blizzards and dust storms.
No one thought we could make it, and now that we have made it and proved it was possible.
Perhaps no one wishes to follow in the footsteps that we have fought to make.

Whatever excuse others may make is out of fear, denial and the dread of the hardships of the trial.

Even some of those who called it simple did not go to the end.

We are the Titan Warriors.

Self-Discouraged

WHEN YOU ARE WORRIED ABOUT your appearance, the act of self-punishment is the worst, most dangerous, and hardest punishment to prevent.

The insecurity about a few gained pounds that you feel that you must lose or being anorexic and fighting to loose only a few more inches.

Not smiling for fear that everyone will stare at your braces or imperfect teeth, is a mental insecurity of not fitting in. We become unhappy with our face for what we think are flaws.

A hatred for having to wear eyeglasses, being unable to hear, or having to use a wheelchair.

Some flaws are easily covered but once one problem is gone another one will always takes its place. If you are comfortable in your own skin perhaps others will be more accepting to.

We look at ourselves by how others see us and others see us by how we see ourselves. Some people use objects to hide how they feel about themselves. We are our own worst critic. If you are confident and comfortable with yourself nothing can stop you. The powerful strength that is within our heart is often held back by our own fear of taking a first step.

The powers we all hold are hidden until the day we become aware of what we hold in our hands. Concentrate on your strengths to help pull you out of your own fear. Those with a hatred for themselves do not see themselves as special, they are like butterflies who have never even see the beauty of their wings, but that doesn't stop them from living their life. It does not discourage them when they see the bright colors of other butterflies even though they cannot see their own wings. Even the plainest moth opens its wings to show its colors, and the powerful wind doesn't hold them back from getting to their destination.

What voices have crumbled your fragile building of talents and overcome challenges of your own goals? Never let the feeling of being overwhelmed take over and destroy your confidence. Why do words wear you down and guilt pulls on your heart? What is your self-worth?

Your strength can pull you through the hard days, so don't let a voice from within you scare you from learning. Even if you fall and fail, what is lost?

We all at times make mistakes. That is how we grow and learn and it will make you a better and stronger person when you try again.

The Run Down House

THERE IS AN OLD RUNDOWN house on a hill. The wallpaper had sunken and fallen as well as there were fist sized holes in many of the walls. Many clumps of dust had gathered in the corners, like ants in a colony, and the black and white photos in the hallway were dull with dust. A smell of incense and of mold, also the high humidity of the past, had claimed its place in the house while now a cool breeze came through the gaping holes which had held window panes many years ago. Particles of dust floated across the room in the air as if they were dancing to a song, appearing and disappearing between the sunlight and shadows. As I gazed at the holes in the walls, I saw a maze of ant and termite tunnels that were still active with movement.

The food in the creaky cupboards, that had expired long ago, was also covered with dust. The rusted pump jack in the kitchen no longer pulled clean water out of the rocky ground below, but a brown sewage like substance which had a smell of rust to it. A cast iron stove still had its place in the living room. It seemed to make the house cozy and inviting which contradicted the smell of dead mice in the room. Light came through the unkempt roof, and the floor creaked with every shoe print that I had just left behind.

The handmade oak desk had a dust covered novel on it which had been turned to page thirty-six. As I touched the novel with my fingertips I closed my eyes and thought back to a time when I had lived here with my parents 40 years ago. Tears started to form in the corner of my eyes as memories flooded into my mind, like it was yesterday rather than so many years ago.

A faded photo of a family in suits and dresses was on the corner of the wooden desk in the bedroom. My thoughts, at this time, were like a scrapbook of memories whirling through my mind. Among the things, that I remember, was my grandmother saying,

"Every building has a story to tell for every day since it was built."

Oh if this RUN DOWN HOUSE could only talk.

Broken Relations

Would you cry for me if I did not return?
Or would you stand and watch me burn?
Would you turn and leave if you had a choice?
Because of you I now have a voice.

If I had not seen the door.
I would have fallen to the floor.
Pushed to the cliff where I saw my ghosts.
You are the one I loved the most.

My past being covered in the present.
The sun now gone all's viewed as a crescent.
The way that you gave me all of the fault.
You never thought walking away would be the result.

Reality Faded Adrenaline

The thrill of hijacking yet another car.
The adrenaline rush of shoplifting.
A strong temptation for illegal drugs.
The controversial fight in your head, for
that one more harmless drink of alcohol.

THE BEATING OF YOUR RACING heart and the fading of reality begins to surround you. You have told yourself every time that this will be the last thrill and the last bottle of alcohol.

Unstopped temptations overtake the mind, body, self-respect, and at times a life as well. The fight between the will and the want becomes a long and drawn out fight and it may help to have a friend's supportive hand holding onto your shoulder. Some consequences are lessons from temptations people have attempted. Why do people continue a criminal thrill even though they have to continuously pay the penalty?

Habits are hard to break but until then the world will revolve around whatever is on your mind and what you have done. It starts as fun but as time charges on, you become ignored by friends, and begin to lose the property that you own. As your actions become a part of the past your conscience plays games within you, releasing frustration in yourself and to everyone else that is in your life. A change of heart is harder than a change of mind.

The hardest problems can be resolved if we recognize them. What has influenced us to move forward in the habits of our own problems? Why do we do the things that hurt us mentally, physically, and emotionally and also destroys trust from others and in ourselves? The day you refuse will be your hardest day, but as you become stronger you will always look back to those troubling times fighting not to give in again under stress, a traumatic accident or the longing for that old feeling. To stay away from the thrill gives you more power over yourself and to become strong with self-respect. Whenever you fall back into the old routine you must fight to gather the strength to shake off the feeling that draws you into the gravitational pull of the vortex.

Looking away is always difficult but it is the action that breaks the chain link fence, unless you look back. The actions people grow out of are the ones that they fight to control.

After time you will realize that it was immature and nothing was gained from your actions. Where are the friends now that pushed you into uncomfortable situations in the past? Have they grown up or have they found themselves trapped in a circle of their own problems?

It takes the heart to change the mind but it takes more than the mind to change the heart.

A Letter from the Heart

MY ADMIRATION FOR YOU IS so strong that I would do anything for you. I am unsure if the love between us is mutual, but I will continue to wait for the day I see you again. Our path has separated for now, but I know we will meet once again.

Life doesn't make sense, but I have been waiting, and will forever wait for you. That beautiful smile of yours is embedded into my mind, like wise words, that I try to live my life by.

I wonder what you have been doing lately. I hope your days are enjoyable and your job is what you have always wanted. I wish there were more contact between us than there is now. I am always a call away from you. Even if you meet someone else I will be here for you, whenever you need someone to talk to. I would have preferred it, if you lived closer to me, but the constant reminder of your absence tells me that I have done the right thing by letting you go and chase your dream job, even though it is farther than you have ever traveled before.

My arms are always open for you, the one that I grew up with. Whenever I was with you, it felt right. But now the brightness of my day has turned into night. I wish I were on your mind as much as you are on mine. I am sorry for all that I wasn't able to do, when you were here, but now that you're gone I see my mistakes. I wish there was something that I could do to bring you back to me.

Although I wait, I know that our parallel lives will cross someday again. I will always wonder, "what if, What if I had gone with you, what if I had asked you to stay." Would life be easier than it is now? Now that you are gone I am here writing this letter. I wish it would find you rather than staying in the locked desk in the living room beside the picture of us. If the wind could carry this letter, I would have sent it weeks ago. But you haven't called, and I don't have your address, so I will keep this letter until the day I know where you are.

Take care my love, I will never forget you!

Questions to Forever Ponder

1. Where does love stop between a parent and a child?
2. Where is the respect between the young and the elderly?
3. Why is there peer pressure to be someone you are not?
4. Why do you get judged by people that don't seem to have a voice that matters?
5. Why do lies spread faster than praise?

6. Why is an uncaught liar often loved more than a hard worker?
7. Why does pain pull together loved ones but push away the ones that hate you?
8. Why are mistakes shunned when all they are, are life lessons?
9. Why does homeschooling, in some people's minds, have to lead to illiteracy?
10. Don't all roads lead to learning? Then why does history have to repeat itself?

11. Why don't we learn from our mistakes the first time, rather than continuing to pay for them?
12. Why is it difficult to forgive a childish mistake that may have already been forgotten?

13. Why do physically strong people feel weak and useless when a loved one is in pain?

14. Why is a smile contagious and a growl cause frustration?

15. Even with friends why can you be lonely?

16. Why is showing emotion weakness, when only deceased people are emotionless?

17. Can there be strangers in your family?

18. Is it wrong to look up to famous people and then degrade them for mistakes that are common to others?

19. Why do we let religion destroy friendships?

20. Is getting even worth losing your life over?

21. Is it possible to learn something you thought you already knew?

22. What changes happen to make a marriage fail?

23. Why doesn't hard work always pay?

24. When is someone mature enough to go through life?

25. Why is maturity counted by age?

26. With responsibility comes trust, but if you lose trust what responsibility will you have?

The pursuit of happiness should not be gaged by physical happiness but by mental peace.

Answers to Riddles

Riddle 1
Money

Riddle 2
Love

Riddle 3
Revenge

Riddle 4
Power

Riddle 5
Tsunami

About the Author

Chance Hansen was born and raised in Alberta, Canada. At the age of thirteen, he was asked to write a poem. He found his love for writing after his composition of THE UNSPOKEN SIDE. He balances his baking for Farmers' Markets and helping on the farm where he has been home-schooled since leaving public school in grade three.